July 2011

Steve,

Enjoy the beauty of God's creation!

Love to you always,
Sandy

Genesis - Chapter 1 and 2: 1-4

The Adirondacks

In Celebration of the Seasons

THE ADIRONDACKS

In Celebration of the Seasons

MARK BOWIE

North Country Books
Utica, New York

To
Rushelle ~ a flower and my great joy in all seasons
My parents, sisters, and brother ~ with love

Contents

Beaver in Grampus Lake outlet

Summer garden, Warren County

Preface

As I drove along Route 3 west towards Cranberry Lake on a drizzly autumn morning, dense forest encroached on both sides, the diverse mix of trees forming an intricate mosaic of vibrant colors. Mile after mile, the woods seemed intensely alive, bursting with energy. A familiar feeling of awe welled up from deep within me, and I fell in love with the Adirondacks all over again. It happens every season.

The Adirondacks exhibit a special beauty, unique in character and spirit; a timeless terrain of rugged mountains covered with rich northern forests, spattered with inviting waters. Overlain by four distinct seasons,

Autumn maples, Franklin County

Sand Beach Mountain, Brant Lake

they are a breathtaking tapestry — a feast for the senses — continually evolving throughout the year.

In the seasons we see life adapting to the movements of our earth and sun. These cosmic forces are beyond our control; the seasons progress inexorably, oblivious to us. They sweep across the Adirondack landscape and flow through it, their passage recorded in the foliage, their moods reflected in the waters. A cross section of the High Peaks region in October may show summer greenery lingering along shorelines, blazing autumn colors marching up the mountainsides, snow and ice capping the summits.

Each day reflects fractals of the seasons, moving quickly across the stage, chased by time: sunrise as spring, the blossoming of life; midday like summer, full of light and

activity; dusk like autumn, its colors intense, foretelling darkness; and night as winter, a time of rest before the cycle begins anew.

In their brief spotlight, the seasons unveil new splendors and, even to hardened Adirondackers, inherent challenges. With the trillium, the jack-in-the-pulpit, and the newborn mergansers of spring come mud, ravenous black flies, deer flies, and mosquitoes. Summer's blue skies peppered with white puffy cumulus are often overtaken by violent thunderstorms. Autumn's riotous colors bring a hint of decay and a foreboding sense of warmth's final caress before the descent into nearly half a year of penetrating cold and extended darkness. Yet even then, sunshine on fresh snow transforms barren winterscapes into winter wonderlands.

The seasons redecorate the mountains, woods, and waters with fresh colors and patterns. For us, the scenic possibilities are limitless. And there is something reassuring in the knowledge that forces much larger than us are in control, providing such wealth. There's something of the cosmos in that, something of God. A new season always comes; we can't prevent it. The cycle of the seasons rolls on and on.

Mark Bowie

above *Brandy Pond, near Upper Saranac Lake*

Spring

Explosion of Life

Sometime around the spring equinox, north country life stands poised in anticipation, as do birds before dawn noisily awaiting the sun's appearance. Then suddenly, as winter releases its smothering hold, life exults with unbridled joy. In some six weeks, from late April through mid-June, the forests explode from bare branches to full bloom. As trees and bushes leaf out, the forest floors erupt with ground-covering plants pushing through pine duff and around greening mosses. Snowmelt and frequent rains re-energize rivers, streams, and waterfalls.

Activity abounds. The first showy flowers bloom, attracting pollinators. Bears and burrowers venture from dens. Newborns are weaned. Drawn by warmer temperatures, blossoming food supplies, and instinct we little understand, loons and other waterfowl return from their southern wintering sites to the same lakes and ponds on which they were raised. Another migration occurs simultaneously: seasonal homeowners come to prepare their camps for the new year, and the woods resound with pounding hammers and whirring saws.

It's spring, a time of rebirth and renewed hope — the season of anticipation — a miraculous explosion of life, sound, and color.

opposite *Star flower, Chestertown*
previous pages *Pink lady slippers near Lake Eaton*

above *Moth on False Solomon's Seal*
opposite *Adirondack guideboat at St. Regis Pond outlet*

above *Budding maples near Hague*
opposite *Clear Pond, Elk Lake, and the High Peaks from Clear Pond Mountain*

17

The spring forest blooms delicately with an astounding assortment of soft green hues: creamy greens, olive-greens, phosphorescent lime-greens, yellow-greens. They mingle with leaves of white, beige, yellow, and gold. Maples bud burnt-orange and russet red. Even evergreens sprout new needles — velvety soft — as if shedding last year's coat for a new spring wardrobe. It's a forest bouquet, seemingly the reciprocal pastels of autumn's vibrant primary colors. It blooms only a few short weeks, yet radiantly.

Waterfall and spring foliage on Eleventh Mountain

above *Dew drops on bluets near Elk Lake*
opposite *Stewart Creek, Luzerne*

21

above *Cold River, High Peaks Wilderness*
opposite *Cardinal flowers along Glen Creek*

above *Blue flag iris near Cranberry Lake*
opposite *Tulips in a Sagamore Hotel garden, Bolton Landing*

above *In an annual rite of spring, Loon Lake fishermen attract bullhead with a campfire*
opposite *Loon Lake sunrise, Warren County*

Summer

Green on Green

The multicolored pastels of Adirondack spring forests slowly evolve into remarkably monochromatic green-on-green summer plumage. It will remain so from July into mid-August, then progressively diverge into new hues as the autumnal equinox approaches.

Blue skies, pleasant temperatures, a balmy breeze wafting off the lake, the fresh scent of pine and balsam, mountaintop views of ever more mountains rolling to the horizon, the sounds of children playing at the beach — all color our idyllic memories of an Adirondack summer. The weather, often magnificent, is also volatile, with searing heat, sweatshirt nights, storms, and drought. The blue-sky days can be followed by a hazy stretch of ninety-degree temperatures with ninety-percent humidity. Rainstorms are frequent; thunderheads billow to great heights, lit with dramatic stormlight, packing heavy rains, lightning, and strong winds. All-day soakers — torrential downpours reminiscent of spring rains — make souvenir shoppers of sun worshippers.

But for three enchanted months, the Adirondacks are their most hospitable. The woods are hiked, the mountains climbed, the waters paddled. S'mores and memories are made; camp traditions begun under the summer sun are passed down through generations.

opposite *Misty sunrise over Lower St. Regis Lake inlet, Paul Smiths*
previous pages *Hiker resting atop Round Mountain, with a view of the High Peaks*

above *Sailboats on Silver Bay, Lake George*
opposite Minne Ha Ha *passengers viewing the southern Lake George waterfront*

36

above *Champlain Valley wildflowers beneath storm clouds, looking east towards the High Peaks*
opposite *Canada geese beneath storm clouds, Fish Creek Ponds*

above *Bald eagle perched above Fish Creek*
opposite *Canoe on a Rollins Pond island*

Wildflowers in Profusion

The explosion of life which began in spring continues to flourish — Adirondack life at maximum force. Wildflowers adorn the meadows and roadways: Indian paintbrush, asters, daisies, lilies, goldenrod, Queen Anne's lace, purple clover, thistle, and more. On the mountaintops, Arctic vegetation sprouts from thin soils scraped by ancient glaciers from bare bedrock. Around lakes and ponds, arrowhead, purple pickerelweed, and white and pink water lilies bloom; pitcher plants, sundew, cotton grass, bog and sheep laurel, rosemary, and cranberry decorate the boreal bogs. On foggy mornings, dewdrops glisten on spider webs strung between the tamaracks and black spruce.

For now, seemingly, life celebrates having pulled abreast the elusive seasons. The forests ring with the melodies of songbirds and the jackhammering of woodpeckers. Deer, foxes, bears, and a variety of smaller mammals, amphibians, and reptiles patrol the understory. Eagles, great blue herons, kingfishers, Canada geese, and loons fish the waters. For plants and animals, the time of plenty is short. Changes lie just over the horizon.

Wildflowers in a marsh near Upper Saranac Lake

above *Cedar waxwing snatching a moth in mid-air above the St. Regis River*
opposite *Tiger lilies on Hackensack Mountain, Warrensburg*

above *Sunrise over Whiteface Mountain and the McKenzie Range, from Harrietstown*
opposite *Canoeists on Follensby Clear Pond*

above *Sunrise clouds reflected in Spuytenduivel Brook, near Brant Lake*
opposite *Salmon River summer flow, near Long Lake*

Flock of Activity

Six million visitors flock to the Adirondack Park annually, the great majority between the Independence Day and Labor Day holidays. They come to enjoy recreational activities, to breathe the fresh mountain air and absorb the scenic beauty. They come for fun and relaxation, to be inspired by nature, for spiritual rejuvenation. The major tourist attractions in Old Forge and the villages of Lake George and Lake Placid bustle with activity. Cruise ships full

of sightseers ply the big lakes. Campers crowd the many campgrounds. Hamburger and ice cream stands stay open well into the evening. General stores — quaintly peaceful the other nine months of the year — sell ice, soda, beach towels, and water toys to sunbathers in droves.

As Labor Day weekend comes to a close, the tourists exit en masse; the next influx — on a smaller, more tranquil scale — will sweep in for the dramatic displays of fall foliage.

above *Adirondack chairs at Blue Mountain Lake*

above *Upper Saranac Lake (distant center) and the St. Regis Canoe Wilderness, from St. Regis Mountain*
opposite *Mount Arab fire tower in morning mist*

above *Two-hour exposure of star trails and campfires reflected in Fish Creek Ponds*
opposite *Canoeists on Whey Pond*

above *Common loons on a Franklin County pond*
opposite *Pitcher plants in a boreal bog along Middle Pond, near the St. Regis Canoe Wilderness*

Awash in Color

With the wistful passing of an Adirondack summer comes, arguably, the most glorious time of the year — autumn. The summer commotion is but a memory. The pesky flying bugs have gone dormant. Solitude returns to the North Country. The changing seasons re-dress the landscape; the greens of summer evolve into an artist's palette of luminous yellows, oranges, and reds. The distinctly Adirondack mix of deciduous and evergreen forests at peak color is absolutely breathtaking in clear daylight, blurring to pastel watercolors on misty mornings. Conifers boost the contrast; spruce spires poke above the hardwood canopy like clusters of church steeples — rural New England gone wild.

Marshes typically flare with the first bold colors: maples and vines blaze red; tamaracks glow lime-yellow. As air temperatures cool forest colors change, sweeping from north to south, down from higher elevations and up from cold, fog-shrouded valleys. Vivid colors arrive in mid-September and shimmer through mid-October. Mountaintops, hillsides, valleys — every niche of the landscape — are awash in color. And Adirondack waters are never so boldly clad as on windless days at the height of fall plumage, mirroring the shorelines with immaculate detail.

Autumn lengthens and the waters turn gray and restless, whipped to whitecaps as Arctic cold fronts blow through. The first snow flies. But an outlier of summer provides a reprieve: a period of unseasonably warm weather — Indian Summer — showcases the magnificent foliage. It's a soul-rejuvenating curtain call for beauty before pre-winter chill strips the forests bare.

opposite *Majestic birches, Fish Creek Ponds State Campground*
previous pages *Fall foliage reflected in Round Pond, Dix Mountain Wilderness*

above *Route 30 winds through fall foliage between Long and Tupper Lakes, as seen from Coney Mountain*
opposite *Aerial view of McRorie Lake and parts of Mud Pond (foreground right) and Long Lake (distant right)*

above *Maple leaves on an anorthosite outcrop along the Boquet River*
opposite *Red maples, Warren County*

Rain Paints the Forest

know a place where spirits move the wind, where rain paints the forest and fires the imagination. It's a flank of Swede Mountain, near Brant Lake. Here Nature herself is both the canvas and the artist who paints it.

On overcast autumn mornings I've watched sheets of misty rain splash effervescent colors onto the forested slopes. Every few minutes, fresh squalls would blow through, cleansing the atmosphere, splashing more intensity onto the trees. The lighting was soft, the air intoxicating. I walked the hillside, watching the kaleidoscope change, stopping frequently to compose new tree portraits. I juxtaposed maples with yellow birch and aspen leaves, zoomed in on the rain-blackened trunks and the poetic grace of limbs, the explosion of color surrounding them. It was as if I walked a museum gallery, each composition a natural masterpiece.

Fall foliage on Swede Mountain

above *Adirondack pack basket full of autumn leaves, Chestertown*
opposite *Fallen autumn leaves, Rollins Pond State Campground*

above *Canada geese in Park Lake, near Long Lake*
opposite *Autumn reflections and light rain on Palmer Pond*

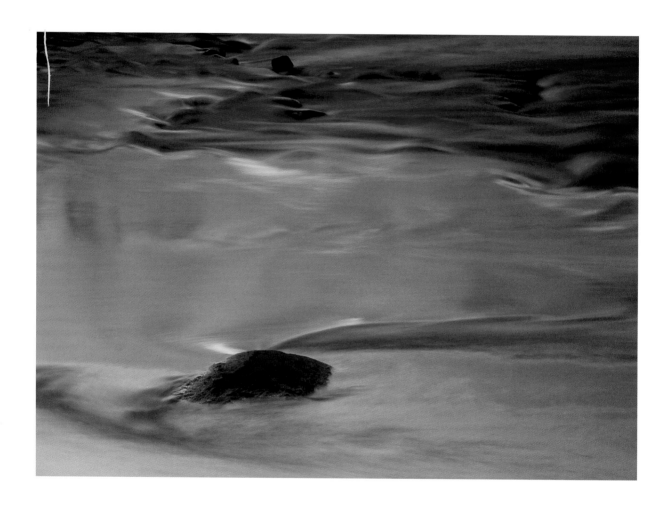

above *Fall reflections in the Raquette River*
opposite *Maple over the Cedar River*

72

South Branch of the Grasse River

Unexpected Beauty

As late autumn gales blow the last colorful leaves off the trees, the forests turn stark and forlorn. The newly fallen leaves, easily dismissed underfoot, decompose in a final blaze of glory. Indicative of the biodiversity of the northern forest, the many leaf species in this image, piled against a breakwater of tree roots, are turning seemingly unearthly colors: crazy pinks, bubblegums, tangerines, aquamarines, and lavenders. There's beauty even in decay.

Roots and fallen leaves, Blue Ridge Wilderness

above *Garnet Hill Lodge hammock*
opposite *Adirondack guideboat on Lake Eaton*

above *Sunrise over Pelky Bay, Upper Saranac Lake*
opposite *Six-hour exposure of airplanes streaking through concentric star trails over Fish Creek Ponds*

79

Winter

White on White

irrus clouds tinged with the teals and yellows particular to winter stream across afternoon skies, heralding year's end. Darkness settles in earlier each day. In the North Country, trees go dormant; new growth won't burst forth for nearly another half year.

Though threadbare, the winter landscape is magical at its extremes. Snow accumulates over one hundred inches most years. Classic Nor'easters, dumping feet of heavy, wet snow, extend winter into late March and April. And it gets cold — very cold. In fact, several days each year, northern and western Adirondack villages are routinely the coldest places in the continental United States. Winter temperatures average about sixteen degrees, and sub-zero readings are common, with a record low of minus fifty-two degrees recorded at Stillwater and Old Forge.

On clear, cold nights the stars seem to sizzle. The air feels brittle; so cold and dry it freezes in our noses and sucks the breath from our lungs. It also does seemingly ominous things to woods and waters. Frozen lakes resound with thundering booms and strange "thwarping" sounds, like wire stretched taut then released, as ice cracks. Trees pop — loud as gunfire — as sap freezes and expands.

Rare episodes of heavy snow followed immediately by bitter cold create spectacular "white-on-white" winterscapes. Entire mountainsides are flocked white, with giant pines poking above frosted hardwoods. I've seen glittering ridges in the Wilcox Lake Wild Forest appear to go on indefinitely — much as Adirondack winters themselves seem to do.

opposite *Side channel of Bog River Falls*
previous pages *Fresh snow on evergreens, Old Forge*

above *Birches in a snowstorm, near the Cascade Lakes*
opposite *Ausable River, Keene*

above *Red pine forest, near the Saranac Lakes*
opposite *Split Rock Falls, Boquet River*

Snow Simplifies the Landscape

There's something charming about falling snow. As it blankets the earth, it softens sounds and smoothes textures, disguising the complexity of the woodlands while accentuating prominent landforms: ridgelines and ledges, rhythmic lines of balsam and spruce poised like sentinels. Blue-sky days following a fresh snowfall transform the landscape into a fairyland setting: sun-struck diamonds glisten on the snow; the air is crystal clear, the snowbound trees perfectly uniform, as in a cartoon.

The snow and ice entice skiers, skaters, snowmobilers, sledders, snowshoers, and ice fishermen to explore an Adirondack Park so different from the one they know in other seasons. They've discovered that, for those who bundle up and get outdoors, the winter landscape is a vast natural playground.

Boreas River, Vanderwhacker Mountain Wild Forest

above *Looking northeast over the south basin of Lake George*
opposite *Nordic skaters on Lake Champlain, near Split Rock Mountain*

above *Snowmen and Giant Mountain, St. Huberts*
opposite *Barn and snow-capped Mount Marcy (left), Mount Colden (middle), and Algonquin Mountain (right)*

93

above *Thirty-six inches of fresh snow, Chestertown*
opposite *Night blizzard, Old Forge. Pink streaks are automobile taillights, yellow streaks are snowmobile headlights*

above *Ice shanties on Lake Champlain, Crown Point*
opposite *Mallards on the Schroon River, Warrensburg*

Seasons in Transition

The Mists of Change

The seasons blend gradually, overlapping like images in a slide show — one dissolving as the next eases in. Yet drastic changes often confound the natural order: rogue snows dust spring blossoms and peak fall foliage; an unforeseen heat wave sends spring campers swimming; raw autumn days misplaced in August bring driving winds that make ponds run like rivers.

The transitions between seasons are marked with movement: lakes and ponds freeze or thaw; animals cache food supplies and prepare dens; birds flock, preparing to migrate. Even the atmosphere gets restless. Air masses, warming or cooling more quickly than the slowly modulating lands and waters they pass over, generate mists and fog. They are mists of change: ethereal, fleeting as the seasons themselves. In late winter, fog enshrouds the forests as unseasonably balmy air melts the remaining snow. On September mornings, plumes of fog rise from lakes and ponds; fleecy rolls hover over river valleys. The fog suffuses the landscape with the pastel blues of the sky and greens of the forest. These "blue-green" mornings are soft and tranquil, the blending of seasons sublime.

opposite *Ice-capped Blue Mountain and Lake Durant*
previous pages *Little Pond outlet, Johnsburg*

above *Waterfowl flying over misty Loon Lake, Warren County*
opposite *Snow on autumn swamp, near the St. Regis Canoe Wilderness*

above *Ice on newly fallen autumn leaves, near Henderson Lake*
opposite *Fresh snow on fall foliage, Floodwood Road near Saranac Inn*

Runaway Arctic Freight Train

Vanderwhacker Mountain, late October. My hiking partner, Mark Lindsay, and I had been enveloped in fog and buffeted by strong summit winds for over an hour. We bided our time, hoping a break in the weather would unveil what local guidebooks touted as the best view of the High Peaks from anywhere in the southern Adirondacks.

A tiny pond suddenly appeared far below us, glinting in sunlight. As we scrambled up the fire tower, the clouds parted, revealing a stunning 360-degree panorama: massive mountains rimmed the horizon; lakes and ponds glistened amongst rolling foothills carpeted by an autumn forest mosaic; silvery streams wound amongst them.

The clouds continued to lift, but now snow squalls lashed the tower from the west — a runaway Arctic locomotive pulling a seemingly endless line of freight cars, spilling their icy cargo on mountains, woods, waters, and us as they barreled overhead.

The scenery moved as if alive. Cloud shadows swept across the forests. Rainbows, snowbows, and fogbows materialized, then dissipated as the mists scurried on. The sun threw brilliant "God beams" through dark storm clouds, highlighting the waters with angelic white light. Likewise, the mountains were alternately cast in purple-blue shadow, then illumined with sun fire.

Caught between two seasons, we spent two exhilarating hours recording the drama. Later that night our faces glowed with windburns, our souls with wonder.

Snow squalls over mountains east of Long Lake, from Vanderwhacker Mountain

above *Pre-dawn mists, Raquette Lake*
opposite *Goldenrod along Tupper Lake*

Nighttime drops a cloak of anonymity over the Adirondack landscape; mountains and forests merge into a single silhouette. Above, the indigo sky is dotted with distant constellations and brilliantly beaming planets. The moon launches itself into its trajectory. When waters are still, you can actually see reflections of celestial objects bobbing lambently on their black surfaces. Loons shriek their haunting calls to one another — the sounds of northern wildness. The landscape is magical at night.

Darkness envelops us in the eternalness of the Universe and we become pure feeling extended into space. We feel an integral part of its vastness, closer to the Creator. At night our cameras can record physical phenomena beyond our eyes' ability, effectively extending our range of sight and the limits of our perception. They capture light waves emitted by distant celestial objects eons ago, documenting the passage of time.

Four-hour exposure of star trails reflected in Square Pond

Seasons in Time

O ver the course of a year, the daily play of light and the imprint of seasons present the Adirondack landscape in untold guises. The backwoods road, not particularly photogenic in early spring, is surrounded with color and a marvel of composition come autumn. The monotone green mountainsides seen from a peak in summer separate into individual tree species, with definition and character, from that same vista in the fall. A balsam spruce, anonymously entangled in autumn hardwoods, garners the spotlight in winter, dark green and regal against the barren white backdrop. Yet even with the seasonal variety, this landscape somehow retains a distinctive feel that's uniquely Adirondack.

The seasons invite us to see this place afresh, to rekindle our connection to it. They remind us just how ephemeral, how fragile, the Adirondack landscape is. The beauty we see today should not be taken for granted; it is constantly subject to change, by forces beyond us and within us.

opposite *Blue Ridge Road in October and March*
previous pages *McRorie Lake from Mud Pond Mountain in June and October*
(Mud Pond on far right; sections of Long Lake in distant left and right)

above and opposite *Aerial views of Long Lake in June and October*

right and opposite
*Cabin on Minerva Lake
in July and October*

above and opposite *Hornets' nest above Blue Ridge Falls in early September and two weeks later*

above and opposite *Spruce in dense forest, Warren County, in October and March*

above and opposite *Floodwood Road, near Saranac Inn, in June and October*

above and opposite *Cliffs above Lower Cascade Lake in May and December*

above and opposite *Island in a backwater of Loon Lake, Warren County, in August and December*

Special Moments

Special Moments

Awaiting sunrise from the shore of Lake Eaton, I struggled to envision an image that would express the magnificence of autumn in the Adirondacks. Green reeds grew in the shallows; a line of fog billowed over the far side of the lake — promising, but even with sunrise imminent, the scene lacked something meaningful; it didn't necessarily say Adirondack autumn. An orange maple leaf fell on my shoulder and I realized then that many leaves had fallen onto the reeds. As the sun crested the horizon, it backlit the reeds and set the leaves aglow. For added effect, two ducks rounded a boulder just beyond the reeds. One of the resulting images became the cover of this book.

Similarly, as I was photographing candy-stripped fall foliage reflections in the Raquette River, just minutes before the group I was with had to depart, a breeze blew leaves onto a boulder in the foreground. They complimented the reflections beautifully.

In another instance, as I was photographing a brilliant field of goldenrod and asters with Whiteface Mountain as the backdrop, a monarch butterfly — little seen here in recent years — landed on a flower. Click! Then there was the time, as I stood atop a roadside guardrail overlooking the much-photographed outlet of Grampus Lake, wondering how I could possibly make a unique image, a beaver swam out from below me, motoring towards his dam. What timing!

Serendipitous moments like these — when several events unite perfectly before our eyes — are truly special. For in these seminal instances nature affirms what we know in our hearts to be good and true and right. And we appreciate this place even more.

opposite *Raquette River reflections*
previous pages *Morning mists rising from Raquette Lake*

above *Brant Lake*
opposite *Monarch on aster, near Donnelly's Corner*

above *Great blue heron with catfish*
opposite *Pray Road Extension, near Port Kent, Champlain Valley*

above *Fiery sunset on Blue Mountain Lake;* opposite *The same sunset reflected in vacation cabin windows*
following page *Common loon drying its feathers*

Acknowledgements

I am grateful to the many people and organizations who helped with the production of this book, who assisted me in the field, and generously lent their time, knowledge, and support. I thank Rob Igoe, Jr., of North Country Books for believing in this project and guiding it to fruition, and Zach Steffen for collating my images and words into this artistic presentation.

I thank the editorial staff of *Adirondack Life* magazine, past and present, for supporting my photography and writing: Betsy Folwell, Annie Stoltie, Kelly Hofschneider, Matt Paul, Galen Crane, Mary Thill, and Lisa Richmond. I'm also indebted to Dick Beamish and Phil Brown of the *Adirondack Explorer*; Mark Frost and Sandy Hutchinson of *The Chronicle*; Ann Hough of the Adirondack Mountain Club; the Adirondack Council, and the Adirondack Nature Conservancy for supporting my work.

I extend my love and thanks to my Dean Color Photography family — Richard Dean, Everett Bowie, and Wendy Chitty — who set a high standard for quality work and lent me their valuable equipment. I give special thanks to my parents, Everett and Shirley, for their enduring love. Thanks also to my sisters: Ellie, Lesley, Karen, Pamela, and Kristin; their families, and my brother, Michael, for their enthusiasm and support.

For sharing the thrill of discovery with me in the field, I thank Peter Hornbeck of Hornbeck Boats, Adirondack guide Gary "Griz" Caudle, Deborah Caudle, Tim Caudle, Dave Cilley of St. Regis Canoe Outfitters, Mike Prescott, Rick Rosen, Mark Lindsay, Tom McGuire, Nina Schoch of the Adirondack Loon Interpretive Program, Bill Frenette, Jim Frenette, Chris Jerome, Helen Whitaker, Paul Ruest, and Ted Brothers.

And my utmost love and admiration to my wife, Rushelle, whose love enhances my life.

To the wild Adirondacks ~ May they flourish in perpetuity